D0575126

Look at a Tree

Written by Eileen Curran

Illustrated by June Goldsborough

Troll Associates

Library of Congress Cataloging in Publication Data

Curran, Eileen.
   Look at a tree.

   Summary: Text and illustrations describe the
different things that can be seen in or around various
types of trees.
    1. Trees—Juvenile literature. [1. Trees]
I. Goldsborough, June, ill. II. Title.
QK475.8.C87   1985   582.16   84-8843
ISBN 0-8167-0349-3 (lib. bdg.)
ISBN 0-8167-0350-7 (pbk.)

What do you see
when you look at a tree?

Do you see a hive with buzzing bees?

Do you see a nest with eggs?

What else do you see?

Do you see little round cherries

. . . and juicy red berries? What else do you see?

Do you see apples?

What else do you see
when you look at a tree?

Do you see a swing?

Whoops! Can you find a kite in the branches?

What do you see
when you look at a tree?

Do you see a house?

Do you see a mouse?

What else do you see?

Do you see blossoms and flowers?

And pine cones?

Do you see coconuts on a sunny island?

What do you see when you look at a tree?

Do you see golden leaves in the fall?

What else do you see?

Do you see bare branches in the winter?

What do you see when you look at a tree?

Do you see a monkey in the jungle?

Do you see a big bear in the forest?

Do you see a little raccoon?
What do you see when you look at a tree?

Do you see me?